SUZANN A

Bullet In Flight

Exclusive distributors:

Book Sales Limited, 8/9 Frith Street, London W1V 5TZ, UK.

Music Sales Corporation, 225 Park Avenue South, New York, NY 10003, USA.

Music Sales Pty Limited, 120 Rothschild Avenue, Rosebery, NSW 2018, Australia.

To the Music Trade only:
Music Sales Limited, 8/9 Frith Street, London W1V 5TZ, UK.

Photography:
Harold E. Edgerton *cover, 10-11, 58, 62-63,* ©1990 Estate of Harold Ed Edgerton, Courtesy of Palm Press Inc.; Geof Kern, *back cover;* Jeff Gold, *1, 34, 39, 70-71;* Pat Gorman, *30;* Nick Vacarro, *19*

Typeset by TGA Communications, Inc.

Printed in England by The KPC Group, South Willesborough, Ashford, Kent

SUZANNE VEGA

Bullet In Flight

SONGS

OMNIBUS PRESS
LONDON · NEW YORK · SYDNEY

CONTENTS

7   Foreword
    Philip Glass

8   Blue Sky and Blood on 10th Avenue
    Suzanne Vega

SONGS

SUZANNE VEGA

12   Cracking
13   Freeze Tag
15   Marlene on the Wall
16   Small Blue Thing
17   Straight Lines
20   Undertow
21   Some Journey
22   The Queen and the Soldier
24   Knight Moves
26   Neighborhood Girls

SOLITUDE STANDING

28   Tom's Diner
32   Luka
33   Ironbound/Fancy Poultry
36   In the Eye
37   Night Vision
38   Solitude Standing
40   Calypso
42   Language
44   Gypsy
46   Wooden Horse (Caspar Hauser's Song)

DAYS OF OPEN HAND

47   Tired of Sleeping
48   Men In a War
51   Rusted Pipe
52   Book of Dreams
53   Institution Green
54   Those Whole Girls (Run in Grace)
55   Room Off the Street
56   Predictions
57   Fifty-Fifty Chance
59   Big Space
60   Pilgrimage

MORE SONGS

SONGS FROM LIQUID DAYS

64   Lightning
65   Freezing

PRETTY IN PINK

66   Left of Center

70   Suzanne Vega: The Cutting Edge of Folk
      Ronald J. Rindo and James Plath

FOREWORD

There are songs which we think we could have written and there are songs which we wish we had written. There are songs which recall for us a time, a place, a person perhaps. Then there are songs which we can't remember hearing for the first time. All are different kinds of songs which, rare enough, can become classics for us. Then there are the songwriters who write them. We may ask ourselves how they are written. Or do they find them, discover them, or remember them for us? Suzanne is one of those rare people touched by the gift for writing or discovering or remembering, however you want to think of it. This is her first published collection, and I think you'll find here some of those songs which will be "classics" for you. I have.

— Philip Glass

BLUE SKY AND BLOOD ON 10TH AVENUE

by Suzanne Vega

When I was growing up I spent five years in Spanish Harlem and ten years on the Upper West Side. The streets were always crowded with different types of people: kids from the projects, white liberals, students from Columbia. But I didn't hang out much. You could find me in my room, or in the park by the river. Facing south on an afternoon and seeing the angles of sunlight gave me a weird sense of orientation. As a child, I felt: "The sun is there. It's high and on my right. I am here. Everything is O.K." As an adult I had stopped going to the park on the weekends, and that feeling rarely, if ever, visited again.

So it was about 4 o'clock on a cold Sunday, and I was out walking downtown. At 10th Avenue and 14th Street, or thereabouts, suddenly the rest of the city fell away, and I felt that same weird sense of orientation. I was in the meat market area.

The buildings in front of me were long and low, and the sky seemed very wide and intensely blue. It was a shock after the relentless verticality of the city behind me. Because of the cobblestone streets, the tin doors with porthole windows like a ship's kitchen, the ivy on the bricks, the river on my right, I thought for a minute I was somewhere else. Cannery Row, maybe.

It was quiet and still, with a lonely feeling. A strange landscape of cool, fat shadows and slices of dazzling sun on tin. Later, when I lived on Horatio Street where the meat market ends, I learned the neighborhood's other moods and faces, but 4 o'clock on a Sunday afternoon is still my favorite time of day there.

If you look past the serene surface, you find clues to the violence beneath. The most obvious are the painted signs, worn and flaking: "Baby Lamb! Young Kid! Fancy Poultry!" "Breasts, Thighs, Hearts, Livers, Wings." "Boxed Beef." Words that in another context can be sensual, or tender, or playfully erotic, here read like pornography or skewered poetry.

The elevated tracks with their big metal beams seem to shelter this empty place. Pigeons roost under these beams, and fly freely where their relatives are slaughtered every day. Little rivers of blood run along the cracks in the sidewalk, mixing with the sawdust. Or your foot is surprised by a skid of animal fat, white and greasy.

It feels like an underworld. If you see anyone, it might be a man with a wool cap and a big belly and a cigar. He doesn't want you looking at him or minding his business. There is an atmosphere of unseen deals, people watching and being watched, violence about to happen.

And at night when the meat shops close, the other "meat shops" open— the transvestites begin peddling after dark. What are they selling, exactly? I'm not sure. Things are displayed, discussed, bargained for and maybe sold in a quick sleight-of-hand; but you see it only from the corner of your eye, as you walk by fast or speed past in a car. Long, thin mincing men, swaybacked and fiercely feminine, parade on the corners, their skinny masculine legs tottering in high heels and ragged pantyhose. Sometimes there is a bonfire, and you see a few of them, with one womanly man dressed in what seems to be a bathing suit and a full-length fur coat, calling to you, laughing, preening, fixing his lipstick. The graffiti read: "Silence = Death." "Linda, I love you. Frank."

In the morning, though, the place bustles. That's the time I'm least familiar with. It's crowded with trucks and truckers—to get anywhere you wind and dodge your way through a thick traffic of men in bloody white aprons and slabs of meat swinging on hooks. By 2 in the afternoon it has settled down. By 4 o'clock it has regained the stoic feeling of an Edward Hopper painting, with calm cubes of color and long rectangular shadows, and a soft, windy rustle of pigeons and the river.

THE NEW YORK TIMES MAGAZINE
NOVEMBER 20, 1988

S O N G S

SUZANNE VEGA
SOLITUDE STANDING
DAYS OF OPEN HAND

CRACKING

It's a one time thing
It just happens
a lot
Walk with me
And we will see
what we have got
ah . . .

My footsteps are ticking
Like water dripping from a tree
Walking a hairline
And stepping very carefully
ah . . .

My heart is broken
It is worn out at the knees
Hearing muffled
Seeing blind
Soon it will hit the Deep Freeze

And something is cracking
I don't know where
Ice on the sidewalk
Brittle branches
In the air

The sun
is blinding
Dizzy golden, dancing green
Through the park in the afternoon
Wondering where the hell
I have been

ah . . .

FREEZE TAG

We go to the playground
in the wintertime
the sun is fading fast
upon the slides into the past
upon the swings of indecision
in the wintertime

in the dimming diamonds
scattering in the park
in the tickling
and the trembling
of freeze tag
in the dark

We play that we're actors
on a movie screen
I will be Dietrich
and you can be Dean

you stand
with your hand
in your pocket
and lean against the wall
You will be Bogart
and I will be
Bacall

And we can only say yes now
to the sky, to the street, to the night

Slow fade now to black
Play me one more game
of chivalry
you and me
do you see
where I've been hiding
in this hide-and-seek?

We go to the playground
in the wintertime
the sun is fading fast
upon the slides into the past
upon the swings of indecision
in the wintertime
wintertime
wintertime

We can only say yes now
to the sky, to the street, to the night
We can only say yes now
to the sky, to the street, to the night

MARLENE ON THE WALL

Even if I am in love with you
All this to say, what's it to you?
Observe the blood, the rose tattoo
of the fingerprints on me from you

Other evidence has shown
that you and I are still alone
We skirt around the danger zone
and don't talk about it later

Marlene watches from the wall
her mocking smile says it all
as she records the rise and fall
of every soldier passing

But the only soldier now is me
I'm fighting things I cannot see
I think it's called my destiny
that I am changing

Marlene on the wall

I walk to your house in the afternoon
by the butcher shop with the sawdust strewn
"Don't give away the goods too soon"
Is what she might have told me

And I tried so hard to resist
when you held me in your handsome fist
and reminded me of the night we kissed
and of why I should be leaving

Marlene watches from the wall
her mocking smile says it all
as she records the rise and fall
of every man who's been here

But the only one here now is me
I'm fighting things I cannot see
I think it's called my destiny
that I am changing

Marlene on the wall

SMALL BLUE THING

Today I am
a small blue thing
Like a marble
or an eye

With my knees against my mouth
I am perfectly round
I am watching you

I am cold against your skin
You are perfectly reflected
I am lost inside your pocket
I am lost against
your fingers

I am falling down the stairs
I am skipping on the sidewalk
I am thrown against the sky
I am raining down in pieces
I am scattering like light
Scattering like light
Scattering like light

Today I am
a small blue thing
Made of china
made of glass

I am cool and smooth and curious
I never blink
I am turning in your hand
Turning in your hand

small blue thing

STRAIGHT LINES

there's a sound
across the alley
of cold metal
touching skin

and you can see
if you look in her window
that she has gone and cut
her hair again

in straight lines
straight lines

those soft golden lights in the morning
are now on her wooden floor
the wind has swept them through the apartment
she won't need them
any more
any more
any more . . .

she's cut down
on her lovers
though she still dreams
of them at night

she's growing straight lines
where once were flowers
she is streamlined
she is taking the shade down
from the light

to see the straight lines
straight lines

she wants to cut through the circles
that she has lived in before
she wants to finally kill the delusions
she won't need them
any more
any more
any more . . .

but there's a sound
across the alley
of cold metal
too close to the bone

and you can see
if you look in her window
the face of a woman
finally alone

behind straight lines
straight lines

UNDERTOW

I believe right now if I could
I would swallow you whole
I would leave only bones and teeth
We could see what was underneath
And you would be free then

Once I thought only tears could make us free
Salt wearing down to the bone
Like sand against the stone
Against the shoreline

I am friend to the undertow
I take you in, I don't let go
And now I have you

I wanted to learn all the secrets
from the edge of a knife
From the point of a needle
from a diamond
from a bullet in flight
I would be free then

I am friend to the undertow
I take you in, I don't let go
And now I have you

I wanted to see how it would feel
to be that sleek
and instead I find this hunger's
made me weak
I believe right now if I could
I would swallow you whole

I would leave only bones and teeth
We could see what was underneath
And you would be free then, free then

I am friend to the undertow
I take you in, I don't let go
and now I have you

I am friend to the undertow
I take you in, I don't let go
and now I have you
ooh

SOME JOURNEY

If I had met you on some journey
where would we be now
If we had met on some eastbound train
through some black sleeping town

would you have worn your silken robes
all made of royal blue?
would I have dressed in smoke and fire
for you to see through

ah . . .

If we had met in some darkened room
where people do not stay
but shadows touch and pass right through
and never see the day

would you have taken me upstairs
and turned the lamplight low?
would I have shown my secret self
and disappeared like the snow

ah . . .

Oh, I could have played your little girl
or I could have played your wife
I could have played your mistress
running danger down through your life

I could have played your lady fair
all dressed in lace like the foam from the sea
I could have been your woman of the road
as long as you did not come back home to me

ah . . .

But as it is, we live in the city
and everything stays in place
instead we meet on the open sidewalk
and it's well I know your face

we talk and talk, we tell the truth
there are no shadows here
but when I look into your eyes
I wonder what might have been here

because if I had met you on some journey
where would we be now?

THE QUEEN AND THE SOLDIER

The soldier came knocking upon the queen's door
He said, "I am not fighting for you any more"
The queen knew she'd seen his face someplace before
And slowly she let him inside.

He said, "I've watched your palace up here on the hill
And I've wondered who's the woman for whom we all kill
But I am leaving tomorrow and you can do what you will
Only first I am asking you why."

Down the long narrow hall he was led
Into her room with her tapestries red
And she never once took the crown from her head
She asked him there to sit down.

He said, "I see you now, and you are so very young
But I've seen more battles lost than I have battles won
And I've got this intuition, says it's all for your fun
And now will you tell me why?"

The young queen, she fixed him with an arrogant eye
She said, "You won't understand, and you may as well not try"
But her face was a child's, and he thought she would cry
But she closed herself up like a fan.

And she said, "I've swallowed a secret burning thread
It cuts me inside, and often I've bled"
He laid his hand then on the top of her head
And he bowed her down to the ground.

"Tell me how hungry are you? how weak you must feel
As you are living here alone, and you are never revealed
But I won't march again on your battlefield"
And he took her to the window to see.

And the sun, it was gold, though the sky, it was gray
And she wanted more than she ever could say
But she knew how it frightened her, and she turned away
And would not look at his face again.

And he said, "I want to live as an honest man
To get all I deserve and to give all I can
And to love a young woman who I don't understand
Your highness, your ways are very strange."

But the crown, it had fallen, and she thought she would break
And she stood there, ashamed of the way her heart ached
She took him to the doorstep and she asked him to wait
She would only be a moment inside.

Out in the distance her order was heard
And the soldier was killed, still waiting for her word
And while the queen went on strangling in the solitude she preferred
The battle
continued on

KNIGHT MOVES

Watch while the queen
in one false move
turns herself into a pawn

Sleepy and shaken
and watching while the blurry night
Turns into a very clear dawn

Do you love any, do you love none
do you love many, can you love one
do you love me?

Do you love any, do you love none
do you love twenty, can you love one
do you love me?

One false move
and a secret prophecy
well, if you hold it against her,
first hold it up and see
that it's one side stone
One side fire
Standing alone among all men's desire
(they want to know)

Do you love any, do you love none
do you love many, can you love one
do you love me?

Do you love any, do you love none
do you love twenty, can you love one
do you love me?

And if you wonder
What I am doing
As I am heading
For the sink
I am spitting out all the bitterness
Along with half of my last drink

I am thinking
of your woman
Who is crying in the hall
It's like drinking gasoline
to quench a thirst
Until there's nothing there left at all

Do you love any, do you love none
do you love many, can you love one
do you love me?

Do you love any, do you love none
do you love twenty, can you love one
do you love me?

"Walk on her blind side"
was the answer to the joke
it's said there isn't a political bone
in her body

she would rather be a riddle
but she keeps challenging the future
with a profound lack of history

Do you love any, do you love none
do you love many, can you love one
do you love me?

Do you love any, do you love none
do you love twenty, can you love one
do you love me?

And watch while the queen
in one false move
turns herself into a pawn

Sleepy and shaken
and watching while the blurry night
Turns into a very clear dawn

Do you love me?
do you love me?
do you love me?
do you love me?
do you love me . . .

NEIGHBORHOOD GIRLS

"We had our
Neighborhood girl, she
Used to hang out, in front of
McKinsey's Bar, and we were
Interested in her, and her
Clientele . . .
We just wonder where she's gone . . . "
"Oh she's gone?"
"Yes, she's gone, gone, gone."

"I think I know your
Neighborhood girl, she
Lives on my street, now, with
Eyes of ice
I've seen her in the morning, when she is
Walking in the sun
And I always thought that she
Looked kind of nice

She spoke to me once
At a party, I think
And I thought at the time
That she had had too much to drink, because she
Said to me, 'There's a backbone gone
And I've got to get it back
Before going on . . . '

And your neighborhood girl
Seems to have resigned
She was looking out at people
From the back of her mind
And before she went off
She spoke to me again
She came up and said,

'You have the eyes of a friend
And there's a razor's edge
That I have lost somewhere
And I would like it back
So if you've seen it anywhere . . .
I've been out for a while
But I'll be back in a bit
I am just walking through the smoke

Finding out if this is it
Because I've got this feeling
That things are going grey
And I'd like to hear a straight line
To help me find my way . . . '

I looked at her
And I did not know what to say.
She had long black hair."

"Must be a different
Neighborhood girl, cause
Ours had blond hair, in front of
McKinsey's Bar
And we were interested in her
And her
Clientele
We just wonder where she's gone . . . "
"Oh, she's gone?"
"Yes, she's gone, gone, gone."

TOM'S DINER

I am sitting
In the morning
At the diner
On the corner

I am waiting
At the counter
For the man
To pour the coffee

And he fills it
Only halfway
And before
I even argue

He is looking
Out the window
At somebody
Coming in

"It is always
Nice to see you"
Says the man
Behind the counter

To the woman
Who has come in
She is shaking
Her umbrella

And I look
The other way
As they are kissing
Their hellos

I'm pretending
Not to see them
Instead
I pour the milk

I open
Up the paper
There's a story
Of an actor

Who had died
While he was drinking
It was no one
I had heard of

And I'm turning
To the horoscope
And looking
For the funnies

When I'm feeling
Someone watching me
And so
I raise my head

There's a woman
On the outside
Looking inside
Does she see me?

No she does not
Really see me
Cause she sees
Her own reflection

And I'm trying
Not to notice
That she's hitching
Up her skirt

And while she's
Straightening her stockings
Her hair
Has gotten wet

Oh, this rain
It will continue
Through the morning
As I'm listening

To the bells
Of the cathedral
I am thinking
Of your voice . . .

And of the midnight picnic
Once upon a time
Before the rain began . . .

I finish up my coffee
It's time to catch the train

LUKA

My name is Luka
I live on the second floor
I live upstairs from you
Yes I think you've seen me before

If you hear something late at night
Some kind of trouble, some kind of fight
Just don't ask me what it was
Just don't ask me what it was
Just don't ask me what it was

I think it's because I'm clumsy
I try not to talk too loud
Maybe it's because I'm crazy
I try not to act too proud

They only hit until you cry
And after that you don't ask why
You just don't argue anymore
You just don't argue anymore
You just don't argue anymore

Yes I think I'm okay
I walked into the door again
Well, if you ask that's what I'll say
And it's not your business anyway

I guess I'd like to be alone
With nothing broken, nothing thrown
Just don't ask me how I am
Just don't ask me how I am
Just don't ask me how I am

IRONBOUND/FANCY POULTRY

In the Ironbound section
Near Avenue L
Where the Portuguese women
Come to see what you sell
With the clouds so low
The morning so slow
As the wires cut through the sky

The beams and bridges
Cut the light on the ground
Into little triangles
And the rails run round
Through the rust and heat
The light and sweet
Coffee color of her skin

Bound up in iron and wire and fate
Watching her walk him up to the gate
In front of the Ironbound schoolyard

"Kids will grow like weeds on a fence"
She says, "they look for the light
They try to make sense
They come up through the cracks
Like grass on the tracks"
And she touches him goodbye

Steps off the curb and into the street
The blood and the feathers near her feet
Into the Ironbound market

In the Ironbound section
Near Avenue L
Where the Portuguese women
Come to see what you sell
With the clouds so low
The morning so slow
As the wires cut through the sky

She stops at the stall
Fingers the ring
Opens her purse and feels a longing
Away from the Ironbound border

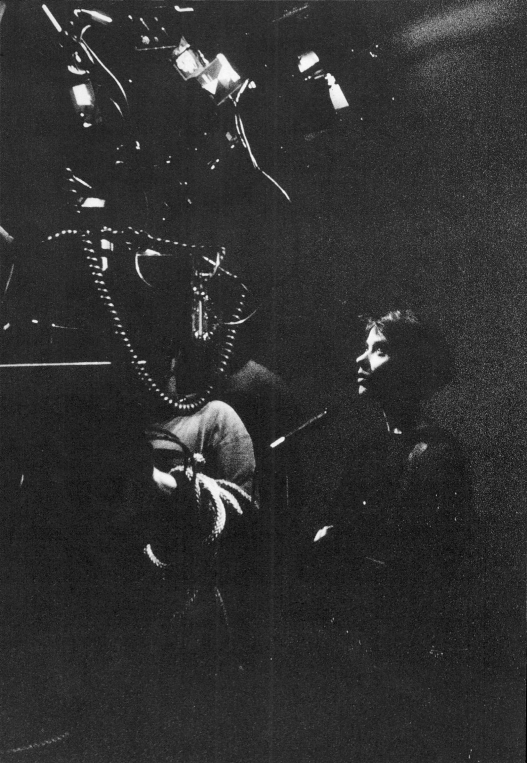

"Fancy poultry
Parts sold here
Breasts and thighs and hearts
Backs are cheap
And wings are nearly
Fancy poultry
Parts sold here
Breasts and thighs and hearts
Backs are cheap
And wings are nearly
Free"
Nearly free
Nearly free

IN THE EYE

If you were to kill me now
Right here I would still
Look you in the eye

And I would burn myself
Into your memory
As long as you were alive

I would not run
I would not turn
I would not hide

I would live inside of you
I'd make you wear me
Like a scar

And I would burn myself
Into your memory
And run through everything you are

I would not run
I would not turn
I would not hide

Look me in the eye
In the eye

NIGHT VISION

By day give thanks
By night beware
Half the world in sweetness
The other in fear

When the darkness takes you
With her hand across your face
Don't give in too quickly
Find the thing she's erased

Find the line, find the shape
Through the grain
Find the outline, things will
Tell you their name

The table, the guitar
The empty glass
All will blend together when
Daylight has passed

Find the line, find the shape
Through the grain
Find the outline, things will
Tell you their name

Now I watch you falling into sleep
Watch your fist uncurl against the sheet
Watch your lips fall open and your eyes dim
In blind faith

I would shelter you
Keep you in light
But I can only teach you
Night vision
Night vision
Night vision

SOLITUDE STANDING

Solitude stands by the window
She turns her head as I walk in the room
I can see by her eyes she's been waiting
Standing in the slant of the late afternoon

And she turns to me with her hand extended
Her palm is split with a flower with a flame

Solitude stands in the doorway
And I'm struck once again by her black silhouette
By her long cool stare and her silence
I suddenly remember each time we've met

And she turns to me with her hand extended
Her palm is split with a flower with a flame

And she says "I've come to set a twisted thing straight"
And she says "I've come to lighten this dark heart"
And she takes my wrist, I feel her imprint of fear
And I say "I've never thought of finding you here"

I turn to the crowd as they're watching
They're sitting all together in the dark in the warm
I wanted to be in there among them
I see how their eyes are gathered into one

And then she turns to me with her hand extended
Her palm is split with a flower with a flame

And she says "I've come to set a twisted thing straight"
And she says "I've come to lighten this dark heart"
And she takes my wrist, I feel her imprint of fear
And I say "I've never thought of finding you here"

Solitude stands in the doorway
And I'm struck once again by her black silhouette
By her long cool stare and her silence
I suddenly remember each time we've met

And she turns to me with her hand extended
Her palm is split with a flower with a flame

CALYPSO

My name is Calypso
And I have lived alone
I live on an island
And I waken to the dawn
A long time ago
I watched him struggle with the sea
I knew that he was drowning
And I brought him into me
Now today
Come morning light
He sails away
After one last night
I let him go.

My name is Calypso
My garden overflows
Thick and wild and hidden
Is the sweetness there that grows
My hair it blows long
As I sing into the wind
I tell of nights
Where I could taste the salt on his skin
Salt of the waves
And of tears
And though he pulled away
I kept him here for years
I let him go

My name is Calypso
I have let him go
In the dawn he sails away
To be gone forever more
And the waves will take him in again
But he'll know their ways now
I will stand upon the shore
With a clean heart
And my song in the wind
The sand will sting my feet
And the sky will burn
It's a lonely time ahead
I do not ask him to return
I let him go
I let him go

LANGUAGE

If language were liquid
It would be rushing in
Instead here we are
In a silence more eloquent
Than any word could ever be
Words are too solid
They don't move fast enough
To catch the blur in the brain
That flies by and is gone
Gone
Gone
Gone

I'd like to meet you
In a timeless
Placeless place
Somewhere out of context
And beyond all consequences

Let's go back to the building (Words are too solid)
On Little West Twelfth
It is not far away (They don't move fast enough)
And the river is there
And the sun and the spaces
Are all laying low (To catch the blur in the brain)
And we'll sit in the silence (That flies by and is)
That comes rushing in and is
Gone (Gone)

I won't use words again
They don't mean what I meant
They don't say what I said
They're just the crust of the meaning
With realms underneath
Never touched
Never stirred
Never even moved through

If language were liquid
It would be rushing in
Instead here we are
In a silence more eloquent
Than any word could ever be
And it's gone
Gone
Gone
And it's gone

GYPSY

You come from far away
With pictures in your eyes
Of coffeeshops and morning streets
In the blue and silent sunrise
But night is the cathedral
Where we recognized the sign
We strangers know each other now
As part of the whole design

Oh, hold me like a baby
That will not fall asleep
Curl me up inside you
And let me hear you through the heat

You are the jester of this courtyard
With a smile like a girl's
Distracted by the women
With the dimples and the curls
By the pretty and the mischievous
By the timid and the blessed
By the blowing skirts of ladies
Who promise to gather you to their breast

Oh, hold me like a baby . . .

You have hands of raining water
And that earring in your ear
The wisdom on your face
Denies the number of your years
With the fingers of the potter
And the laughing tale of the fool
The arranger of disorder
With your strange and simple rules
Yes now I've met me another spinner
Of strange and gauzy threads
With a long and slender body
And a bump upon the head

Oh, hold me like a baby . . .

With a long and slender body
And the sweetest softest hands
And we'll blow away forever soon
And go on to different lands
And please do not ever look for me
But with me you will stay
And you will hear yourself in song
Blowing by one day

Oh hold me like a baby . . .

WOODEN HORSE
(CASPAR HAUSER'S SONG)

I came out of the darkness
Holding one thing
A small white wooden horse
I'd been holding inside

And when I'm dead
If you could tell them this
That what was wood became alive
What was wood became alive

In the night the walls disappeared
In the day they returned
"I want to be a rider like my father"
Were the only words I could say

And when I'm dead
If you could tell them this
That what was wood became alive
What was wood became alive

Alive
And I fell under
A moving piece of sun
Freedom

I came out of the darkness
Holding one thing
I know I have a power
I am afraid I may be killed

But when I'm dead
If you could tell them this
That what was wood became alive
What was wood became alive
Alive

TIRED OF SLEEPING

Oh mom
The dreams are not so bad
It's just that there's so much to do
And I'm tired of sleeping

Oh mom
The old man is telling me something
His eyes are wide and his mouth is thin
And I just can't hear what he's saying

Oh mom
I wonder when I'll be waking
It's just that there's so much to do
And I'm tired of sleeping

Oh mom
The kids are playing in pennies
They're up to their knees in money
In the dirt of the churchyard steps

Oh mom
That man he ripped out his lining
Tore out a piece of his body
To show us his "clean quilted heart"

Oh mom
I wonder when I'll be waking
It's just that there's so much to do
And I'm tired of sleeping

Oh mom
The bird on the string is hanging
Her bones are twisting and dancing
She's fighting for her small life

Oh mom
I wonder when I'll be waking
It's just that there's so much to do
And I'm tired of sleeping

Oh mom
I wonder when I'll be waking
It's just that there's so much to do
And I'm tired of sleeping

MEN IN A WAR

Men
In a war
If they've lost a limb
Still feel that limb
As they did
Before

He lay on a cot
He was drenched in a sweat
He was mute and staring
But feeling the thing
He had not

I know how it is
When something is gone
A piece of your eyesight
Or maybe your vision

A corner of sense
Goes blank on the screen
A piece of the scan
Gets filled in by hand

You know that it was
And now it is not
So you just make do with
Whatever you've got

Men
In a war
If they've lost a limb
Still feel that limb
As they did
Before

If your nerve is cut
If you're kept on the stretch
You don't feel your will
You can't find your gut

And she lay on her back
She made sure she was hid
She was mute and staring
Not feeling the thing
That she did

I know how it is
When something is gone . . . etc.

Repeat to end

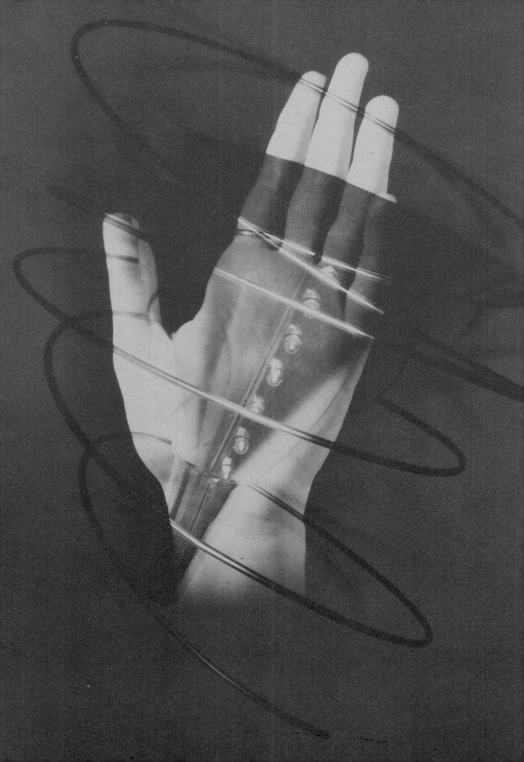

RUSTED PIPE

Now the time has come to speak.
I was not able.
And water through a rusted pipe
Could make the sense that I do.

Gurgle. Mutter.
Hiss, stutter.
Moan the words like water
Rush and foam and choke

Having waited
this long of a winter
I fear I only
Croak and sigh.

Somewhere deep within
Hear the creak
That lets the tale begin.

Now the time has come to move.
I was not able.
Water through a rusted pipe
Could make the moves that I do.

Stagger. Stumble.
Trip, fumble.
Creep along and trickle
Freeze and cough and grip

Having waited
This long of a winter
I fear I only only
Slip and slide.

Somewhere deep within
Hear the creak
That lets the tale begin.

Somewhere deep within
Hear the creak
That lets the tale begin.

BOOK OF DREAMS

In my book of dreams
In my book of dreams
In my book of dreams

I took your urgent whisper
Stole the arc of a white wing
Rode like foam on the river of pity
Turned its tide to strength
Healed the hole that ripped in living

In my book of dreams
In my book of dreams
In my book of dreams

The spine is bound to last a life
Tough enough to take the pounding
Pages made of days of open hand

In my book of dreams
In my book of dreams
In my book of dreams

Number every page in silver
Underline in magic marker
Take the name of every prisoner
Yours is there my word of honor

I took your urgent whisper
Stole the arc of a white wing
Rode like foam on the river of pity
Healed the hole that ripped in living

In my book of dreams
In my book of dreams
In my book of dreams

INSTITUTION GREEN

Institution green
The walls are cracked and dim
And we are standing in a line
Waiting for our faces to be seen

Institution green
Watch the floor and count the hours
None will meet my eye
Private people in this public place

I wonder if they'll take a look
Find my name inside that book
Lose me on the printed page
Where to point the aimless rage

I cast my vote upon this earth
Take my place for what it's worth
Hunger for a pair of eyes
To notice and to recognize

Institution green
A woman stands behind a table
She will call my name
After that I'll be admitted in

I wonder if she'll take a look
Find my name inside that book
Lose me on the printed page
Where to point the aimless rage

I cast my vote upon this earth
Take my place for what it's worth
Hunger for a pair of eyes
To notice and to recognize

Institution green
Teach me how to pull the lever
Push the curtain closed
Take what's needed then just
Let me go

THOSE WHOLE GIRLS
(RUN IN GRACE)

Those whole girls
Hurl down words
Run in packs
With bloom to spare

They know health
Know it well
Skim the cream
And fill the brim

Drip with news
Spin intact
Blaze and stun
And feel no lack

Breathe with ease
Need no mercy
Move in light
Run in grace

Run in grace
Run in grace
Run in grace

ROOM OFF THE STREET

Somewhere in a room
With a poster on a wall
Of a man with his hand
In a fist

Is a woman who's drinking
And her dress is so tight
You can see every breath
That she takes

Every sigh, every sway
You can hear everything that they say
Something's begun like a war
Or a family or a friendship
Or a fast love affair.

The man on the wall
Is his symbol of freedom
It means he has brothers
Who believe as he does

She is moved by
The thing that she sees in his face
When he talks of
The cause

Every sigh, every sway
You can hear everything that they say
Something's begun like a war
Or a family or a friendship
Or a fast love affair.

She leans against him
Her dress is so red
They talk of the salt
And the truth and the bread

The night goes along
The fan goes around
In the room off the street
At the end of the town

Every sigh, every sway
You can hear everything that they say
Something's begun like a war
Or a family or a friendship
Or a fast love affair.

PREDICTIONS

Let's tell the future.
Let's see how it's been done.
By numbers. By mirrors. By water.
By dots made at random on paper.

By salt. By dice.
By meal. By mice.
By dough of cakes.
By sacrificial fire.

By fountains. By fishes.
Writings in ashes.
Birds. Herbs.
Smoke from the altar.

A suspended ring
Or the mode of laughing
Pebbles drawn from a heap
One of these things
Will tell you something.

Let's tell the future
Let's see how it's been done
By dreams. By the features. By letters.
By dropping hot wax into water.

By nails reflecting the rays of the sun.
By walking in a circle.
By red hot iron.
By passages in books.
A balanced hatchet.

A suspended ring or the mode of laughing.
Pebbles drawn from a heap.
One of these things will
Tell you something.

Let's tell the future
Let's see how it's been done.
See how it's been done.

FIFTY-FIFTY CHANCE

50-50 chance
the doctor said
in the cardiac room
as she's lying in bed

there's a pan on the floor
filled with something black
I need to know
I'm afraid to ask

I hug you
I hum to you
I've come to you
I touch you

I tell you
I love you
I sing to you
bring to you
anything

her little heart
it beats so fast
her body trembles
with the effort to last

I hug you
I hum to you
I've come to you
I touch you

I tell you
I love you
I sing to you
bring to you
anything

she's going home
tomorrow at ten
the question is
will she try it again

BIG SPACE

He said you stand in your own shoes
I said I'd rather stand in someone else's
He said you look from your direction
I said I like to keep perspective

Close to the middle of the network
It seems we're looking for a center
What if it turns out to be hollow?
We could be fixing what is broken

Between the pen and the paperwork
There must be passion in the language
Between the muscle and the brainwork
There must be feeling in the pipeline

Beyond the duty and the discipline
I know there's anger in a cold place
All feelings fall into the big space
Swept up like garbage on the week-end

Between the pen and the paperwork
There must be passion in the language
Between the muscle and the brainwork
There must be feeling in the pipeline

All feeling
Falls into the big space
All feeling
Swept into the
Avenues of angles

Between the pen and the paperwork
I'm sure there's passion in the language
Between the muscle and the brainwork
I know there's feeling in the pipeline

PILGRIMAGE

This line is burning
Turning to ash as it hits the air
Every step is a day in the week
It's a Sunday or Monday
A march over months of the year.

This life is burning
Turning to ash as it hits the air
Every death is an end in the race
It's a stopping and starting
A march over millions of years.

Travel. Arrival.
Years of an inch and a step
Toward a source.
I'm coming to you.
I'll be there in time.

This land is burning
Turning to ash as it hits the air
Every line is a place on the map
It's a city or valley
A mark on these miles of fields.

Travel. Arrival.
Years of an inch and a step toward a source.
I'm coming to you.
I'll be there in time.

Travel. Arrival.
Years of an inch and a step
Toward a source.
I'm coming to you.
I'll be there in time.

This line is burning
Turning to ash as it hits the air
Every step is a day in the week
It's a Wednesday or Thursday
A march over months of the year.

Travel. Arrival.
Years of an inch and a step
Toward a source.
I'm coming to you
I'll be there in time.

I'm coming to you
I'll be there in time.

SONGS FROM LIQUID DAYS
PRETTY IN PINK

LIGHTNING

Lightning struck a while ago
And it's blazing much too fast
But give it rain of waiting time
And it will surely pass
Blow over

And it's happening so quickly
As I feel the flaming time
And I grope about the embers
To relieve my stormy mind
Blow over

Shaken this has left me
And laughing and undone
With a blinding bolt of sleeplessness
That's just begun
And a windy crazy running
Through the nights and through the days
And a crackling
Of the time burned away
Burned away

Now I feel it in my blood
All hot and sharp and white
With a whipcrack and a thunder
And a flash of flooding light

But there'll be a thick and smoky
Silence in the air
When the fire finally dies
And I'm wondering who'll be left there

In the ashes of the time
Burned away
Burned away

FREEZING

If you had no name
If you had no history
If you had no books
If you had no family

If it were only you
Naked on the grass
Who would you be then?
This is what he asked
And I said I wasn't really sure
But I would probably be
Cold

And now I'm freezing
Freezing

LEFT OF CENTER

If you want me
you can find me
left of center
off of the strip
in the outskirts
in the fringes
in the corner
out of the grip

When they ask me
"What are you looking at?"
I always answer
"Nothing much" (not much)
I think they know that
I'm looking at them
I think they think
I must be out of touch

But I'm only
in the outskirts
and in the fringes
on the edge
and off the avenue
and if you want me
you can find me
left of center
wondering about you

I think that somehow
somewhere inside of us
we must be similar
if not the same
So I continue
to be wanting you
left of center
against the grain

If you want me
you can find me
left of center
off of the strip
in the outskirts
in the fringes
in the corner
out of the grip

When they ask me
"What are you looking at?"
I always answer
"Nothing much" (not much)
I think they know that
I'm looking at them
I think they think
I must be out of touch

But I'm only
in the outskirts
and in the fringes
on the edge
and off the avenue
and if you want me
you can find me
left of center
wondering about you
wondering about you

SUZANNE VEGA
THE CUTTING EDGE OF FOLK

by Ronald J. Rindo and James Plath

By day give thanks
by night beware
Half the world in sweetness
The other in fear

When the darkness takes you
With her hand across your face
Don't give in too quickly
Find the thing she's erased

from "Night Vision"

When Minimalism first emerged as an art movement in the mid-60's, sing-along, foot-stomping, we-shall-overcome folk music was in its heyday, and singer Suzanne Vega was younger than "Luka," the nine-year-old protagonist in her top-40 song about child abuse. And in the early 70's, when Raymond Carver and others began to adapt the spirit of the visual movement to literature, Vega was still majoring in dance at New York City's famed High School of the Performing Arts. Then came another false start, in literature and theatre at Barnard College. Now, having worked her way up from playing churches and coffeehouses as a solo performer, Vega brings Minimalism to the world of music. Her no-frills lyrics and clean, precise melodies have an edge to them that has cut right through the current folk scene.

"Mostly," says Vega, "what I'm trying to do is look for points of view that I don't think have been uncovered before in songs, and I'm trying to talk about feelings or things that I think are vital, but keep them hard and clear. If I find myself lapsing into sentimentality in my writing, I try to strip it away as quickly as I can. These days I'm trying to use the language as though it were a piece of wood, and I craft it, I hone it down. I sand it, I polish it, and I make sure there are no cracks, no extra pieces or frills that might fall off. I try to keep it as compact as possible. And to me, language is very physical. I feel like I'm sculpting it, like it's a tangible thing. I use words for the way they feel in my mouth, as well as for their meaning."

In the Ironbound section
Near Avenue L
Where the Portuguese women
Come to see what you sell
With the clouds so low
The morning so slow
As the wires cut through the sky

Vega grew up in a house where there was always an acoustic guitar, and both parents were concerned with words. Her Puerto Rican stepfather was a teacher/novelist, while her German-Swedish mother worked as a computer analyst. "There's always a few people who are watching out for how people use language," she says, "and in my family it was always very important." But Vega's imagery and narrative sense are equally sharp, made tense by melodies which rely heavily on minor chords, and a voice which is always on the edge: between whispering and talking, between talking and singing. Sometimes it's a sweet siren-like voice offset by a staccato rhythm, while other times the melody is soothing, and the voice tense. And her subject—the back-alley side of urban life—is something people would rather ignore, even in their daily newspapers.

"In 1981 when I was first beginning to write in that style, audiences weren't used to that subject. If you were playing a folk club they would expect more traditional music, or a sing-along. And instead I would come out and sing 'Cracking'." For those early audiences raised on abstract anthems of love and peace, Vega's music was more unsettling than it was inspiring. But ironically, that has changed. "Now that I sing for a more rock 'n roll crowd, my music is considered to be a sort of gentle alternative . . . which is something I'm not entirely comfortable with either. I would like it to retain its edge and break new ground."

Milwaukee, Wisconsin—In the glitzy, MTV world of 80's pop music, with its extravagant light shows, choreographed videos, and stadium sound systems three stories high, Suzanne Vega is an enigma: an unpretentious singer-songwriter with wit, charm, and an appeal that is rooted in her music and her lyrics.

Described as "New Waif" by Folk City owner Robbie Woliver, Vega's folk-rock is distinctive, the kind of music Joni Mitchell might perform, wrote one critic, if she were also Lou Reed (though Vega lacks Mitchell's feathery soprano and Reed's earthy sexuality). Established and fine-tuned in the folk clubs of Manhattan and Greenwich Village, Vega's musical art is a fusion of her sparkling acoustic guitar work, her hypnotic, vibratoless voice, and her stunningly fresh, poetic lyrics. All three merged beautifully in her concert at the Performing Arts Center on July 14, 1987.

"One thing I remember being struck by as a child—and I listened to a lot of folk music, growing up—was that the songs that were considered the larger issues were very noble, but I didn't feel moved by them. I guess I have this need to be honest about where you come from. I grew up in New York in an ethnic environment, and to me life was hard, and there was no point in pretending that it was like *Leave It To Beaver* when it wasn't.

"If I were to listen to a song about South Africa, I can feel intellectually motivated or I can say, 'yes, apartheid is something we must stop.' But the fact is that I don't come from there. I haven't grown up there, and the things that stir my passion are the things that are more local. And I believe that's how every political movement starts, is with one person having an idea or a deep feeling, and it transforms or can move other people once you have that feeling."

Her debut album, *Suzanne Vega* (A&M Records, 1985), sold 250,000 copies in the United States, and well over a half-million copies overseas, where she became an instant sensation. "Marlene on the Wall" was a top-20 single in Europe, and Vega was suddenly attracting concert crowds of screaming admirers, including, at one point, "2000 drunken Irishmen" who sang along. Although she had the usual dreams of success—Vega quit dancing, in fact, because she felt she wasn't outgoing enough to break out of the chorus line— stardom makes her feel as uncomfortable as she made her first audiences feel in Manhattan folk clubs.

"It's a little disquieting," Vega says. "Suddenly I find I'm a lot more successful than I thought I would be, and it kind of took me by surprise, because people now respond to me as a celebrity. I mean, you have to accept it and be happy for it, but it is a little disquieting, because partly they're responding to the fact that they've read about me in the paper and seen me on television, and this makes them excited to see me on stage." She would, of course, much rather have the audience focus on her music.

> Wearing a black dress, dark nylons, and dark shoes, Vega strolled casually onto the Uihlein Hall stage in front of a four-piece band and bravely opened her show a cappella with "Tom's Diner." Standing in a single dim spotlight, she sang quietly, hands alternately locked behind her back or gently clutching the microphone, like a nervous young girl singing alone for her father at home in the living room. With a little imagination, she might have been a Dickens' character singing for her supper.
>
> But that uneasy, waif-like persona quickly disappeared when she strapped on her acoustic guitar and with the help of her band launched into a two-set show of other songs primarily from her latest album, *Solitude Standing* [A&M, 1987]. She performed standing, without showmanship or racy dance steps, filling the gaps between songs with witty asides and explanations. The crowd remained seated throughout the performance, erupting into applause at the close of each song, then falling into reverential silence when Vega began to speak or sing again.

What makes Vega's music all the more impressive is that she never listened to contemporary music in her youth. "I started singing when I was sixteen, without ever having seen a concert, so I didn't have a clue as to what was out there." When she was nineteen she finally attended her first concert, but only because someone had an extra ticket. She went to see Lou Reed, without knowing who he was. "At first I hated it," she says, "but it stuck with me. Finally I bought *Berlin* and brought it home and listened to it, and it just gave me a hint as to all the stuff that was out there that was valid. I felt suddenly that I could write a song that had a really hard edge to it, as opposed to feeling that I had to make it palatable for the audience." That appropriation has led to others.

Q: Many of the songs from your first album combine medieval and modern imagery. Do you see life in the Middle Ages as a parallel to modern urban life?

A: Well, I think that to some degree when I was writing "The Queen and the Soldier" I was really looking for an archetype—a woman in power. And there really are no archetypal women in power here in America. You know, you can have a teacher or a mother, but it's not the same thing. And somehow a queen seemed to fit it perfectly. I think there's something timeless about some kinds of music and symbols. I mean, I like Gregorian chants. I like to listen to them, and to me they have as much validity, if not more, than other kinds of music that are more contemporary. So I don't have any hesitation about going back to them and taking the elements that I think are really good, and using them in some way. If something's good, it's going to be good no matter what time it's in. I'm not afraid of traveling backwards and forwards. I'm not afraid of mixing contemporary, modernistic, and futuristic things with traditional things. To me it's really vital that you do that, in order to keep the songwriting alive and interesting.

By her own admission, Vega's first songs were "horribly corny," written when she was fourteen. "I was listening to a lot of Woody Guthrie, Pete Seeger, and Cisco Houston—I found this collection of folk music in the thrift shop: it was like someone was throwing out their four-volume set of Folkways music, and so I took it home and listened to it—and so the first song I wrote was a sort-of country song about my youngest brother, how he got into fights, but how I would love him anyway. I remember singing it for my brothers and sisters, and they were not," she laughs, "overly impressed. I guess the second song that I wrote was a long sort-of ballad about a woman who leaves her home to find her freedom, and her father in response commits suicide by drowning in a river. I remember being very pleased with the song; it took me two whole days to write it, and therefore it was really terrific." But she has matured quickly.

As a songwriter, Vega displays freshness and remarkable versatility. The angst-ridden yarns of unrequited love, leftist political propaganda, and whimsical sing-alongs that pepper the repertoire of most folk-singers are absent from Vega's canon. Instead, she offers songs about stifling, urban oppression ("Ironbound/Fancy Poultry"), the ambiguities and inadequacies of language ("Language"), and the complex emotional riddle of love and war ("The Queen and the Soldier"). Her lyrics are marked by an intensity and economy of expression, a storyteller's grasp of the dramatic, and best of all, the intellectual depth and subtlety of fine poetry.

"Each one is different," says Vega, "but usually it begins with the seed of an idea . . . and then I aim for the perfect idea of the song in my mind, which sounds a bit abstract. But when I wrote 'Cracking,' for example, I thought, I really want to write a song called 'Cracking.' All I had was the title, and I wanted to write it from the point of view of a woman who was cracking, but I didn't want to stand on stage and say, 'Oh my God, I'm falling apart!' Instead I wanted to describe a landscape that was like the woman's inner state, and to me it was very exciting to come up with the idea of having her say, 'And something is cracking, I don't know where,' because it was obvious that *she* was cracking."

Q. In your first album there's an air of escapism, and cinematic references that do not appear in your second album.

A: Yeah, I guess that's true. I think it's partly because I was working a day job and rather wistfully watching every Marlene Dietrich movie I could get my hands on on Saturday nights . . . and also trying to find my own identity in the Village, and to some degree being frustrated with my life: working a day job, and having these yearnings to be bigger than life. In the last two years I've grown somewhat. Now instead of playing Dietrich or Bacall, I can play myself. Like the last video I did, I get to play Solitude as a character, which was really exciting because I get to plan her down to the last detail: what she's going to wear, what kind of make-up, what kind of hair . . . .

Q: There does seem to be a shift to dramatic monologues in your second album. Have you been influenced at all by Robert Browning?

A: Not Browning, but definitely T.S. Eliot. I remember for me it was a huge deal when I could finally understand what "The Love Song of J.

Alfred Prufrock" was all about. And this is through the theatre, because I had a teacher who would not allow us to come onstage with anything other than Shakespeare or Eliot as monologues. We couldn't do anything contemporary at Barnard, so I got very deeply into T. S. Eliot because I didn't feel like doing Shakespeare.

Vega is still excited by the discovery of new personas, and sees a connection between her two albums that listeners might miss. "I wasn't using character in the first album as much as I was using the voices of things," she says. "Like 'Small Blue Thing' . . . I was trying to write and sing in the voice of a small blue thing. With 'Undertow,' some people think, Oh, she's being really sexual, or aggressive. But what I was thinking of was a real undertow. What would an undertow say if it were going to sing a song? Which seems rather simplistic or childlike, but it was a fascinating idea to me. I think that the small blue thing and undertow are aspects of myself, just as Luka and Caspar Hauser and Calypso. There's always some sort of emotional parallel, even though the specifics of the circumstances might not be the same. So those songs are also saying something about myself. I'm not saying *what* they're saying—I'm not sure that I know, sometimes, I pick these characters for a certain reason, and I'm not even sure what the reason is. I feel a sympathy for them, or I feel like they say something about myself in some way, but I always feel they're shy with the audience."

She has been a practicing Nichiren Shoshu Buddhist—the family's religion—for thirteen years, and to some extent this has shaped her music. "I think it's a mistake to treat your audience as though they're your best friend, to tell them all these details about yourself that they may not want to know . . . so therefore, I put it in a form that I think they can respond to, and a form that takes it outside of myself.

"Buddhism has affected the way I perceive the world, which to some degree affects how I write. Partly because I'm a Buddhist is why I don't write confessional songs: I mean, you chant in the morning and the evening, and you go to the Buddhist meetings, and you hear other people's experiences . . . and you realize that most people want the same things, or similar things out of life. And I think that was a big step for me, in learning that. Before that I felt very isolated, and I felt like I had suffered more than anyone else on earth—you know, a very sort of adolescent thing—but I think it made me more likely to want to put my songs in a story form, as opposed to a confessional *I am feeling like this* writing."

The beams and bridges
Cut the light on the ground
Into little triangles

And the rails run round
Through the rust and heat
The light and sweet
Coffee color of her skin

Bound up in iron and wire and fate
Watching her walk him up to the gate
In front of the Ironbound school yard

Says Vega, "Language is a difficult thing. I remember being a kid, and my father would ask me how I was feeling about something, and it would take me half-an-hour to begin to talk about how I felt, you know? I would just sit there for half-an-hour quietly because I couldn't find the words to begin with, but I remember always having that frustration." One of the reasons that two years separated her albums was that Vega was wrestling with language. "It's very frustrating," she says, "but I guess I feel it's my job to get as close as I can to the source of actual experiences. I've heard it argued that your experience is shaped by your language, or that you don't really have any experience without language—which I disagree with. There are things that people experience all the time that there are no words for. And so therefore, my job as a writer is to experience these things and find a way to translate them into language, which means stripping away all cliches or things I might have heard in the past to express these things, and just go back to the original source, which is experience, your direct contact with the world. It's as though I'm an animal with no language, and I have to translate my experience into words."

Introducing "Language," Vega noted that words are often incapable of expressing what we feel, what we are trying to explain, that they are "just the crust of the meaning/with realms underneath." In that short lyric she captures the essence of Platonic metaphysics, the notion that with our language we live in the world of shadows, while the Truth rests unapproachable in the world of forms.

Other songs belie her literary training. "Night Vision" was inspired by "Juan Gris," a poem in French by Paul Eluard. "Calypso" is the temptress from Homer's Odyssey in which Odysseus comes from the sea and stays on an island with her for seven years before leaving. Introducing the hauntingly beautiful "Wooden Horse [Caspar Hauser's Song]" Vega explained that Hauser was a boy who spent the first seventeen years of his life in a basement in 18th century Germany. Vega puts herself in Hauser's character, imagining his perceptions of that experience: "In the night the walls disappeared, In the day they returned." In the song, after seventeen years of clutching a small, wooden toy horse, Caspar Hauser emerges and discovers that "what was wood became alive."

"Many of the personas are rather defensive," Vega admits. "But in a song like 'Luka,' for example, I think I give a voice to people who are in that situation, and that's being validated by a lot of the letters I've gotten and people who've come up to me saying, 'You have sung how I have felt' . . . which makes me feel that therefore I'm not just writing a defensive song, but I'm writing from a point of view that needed to be expressed. And when I write a song like 'In the Eye,' I do hope that I'm writing it from the deepest place inside of me, and so therefore it will correspond to someone else's. It disturbed me at first that I never wrote in that song, 'I would fight you back, or pick up a stick and hit you with it'—which I might, in real life—but it just seems to me that if you make someone acknowledge that you're a person, and not a chair or a piece of wood or an object in the environment to be moved around, then it may get all the much harder for them to do whatever it is that they're doing to you, whether it's killing you, abusing you, or whatever. So I think that's at the heart of almost all the songs. To try and assert that feeling of being a human being and being alive, having choices and having freedom. See, to me a lot of the songs are not depressing. The song about Caspar Hauser is very liberating, in a way; it's a song about a person who felt like a thing and became alive, a person who felt like an animal and became a human being . . . with all those dangerous things that happen when you're a person."

She steps off the curb and into the street
The blood and the feathers near her feet
Into the Ironbound market

"Undertow" is still Vega's personal favorite, because it expresses her desire to say a great deal with the least amount of words, images, and narrative elements. "The lines I like best are 'I wanted to learn all the secrets from the edge of a knife, from the point of a needle, from a diamond, from a bullet,' because I'm always trying to learn the secrets from the edge of a knife; I'm always trying to condense and become more economical. It holds true for the writing, and it also holds true for my characters. I intend for a lot of my songs to have many layers of meaning. Like "Ironbound," for example. I could have written a whole album about what it means to be bound by iron, married, or to be confined by your small town, to be a weed and entrapped in netting, any kind of grille . . . It's a common urban image to see living things trying to grow up in a very inflexible environment."

Q: When you were studying literature, which writers spoke to you? Which helped shape your own writing?

A: D.H. Lawrence. I liked his writing because it seemed to be able to evoke certain feelings in you as you were reading it. And he did that by repeating some of his phrases, and by his language. He was very aware of the currents that pass between people in sort of unspoken ways, which was very impressive to me. There's something very liquid about his writing; it's very atmospheric.

And then the other writer that I really liked, who was sort of the direct opposite of that, was John Steinbeck, who was always very clear and sharp, and his characters were always realistic and down-to-earth. At least they were sort of drawn clearly from the outside, whereas D.H. Lawrence's were always drawn clearly from the inside.

In "Night Vision," a song about a mother who sings advice to her child before watching him fall asleep, the philosophy behind Vega's own somber atmospheres and earthy characters emerges. "You'd like to protect people from the things that are out there, but you can't always, so it's better to teach them how to see the dangers and the bad things, and to deal with them and not pretend that they don't exist. That's a problem with a lot of people in America. You don't allow yourself to feel things as complexly as human beings can feel them."

Perhaps because of the confident feminine stoicism apparent in so many songs, but particularly evident in "Calypso" and "In the Eye," Vega appeals, if one can draw any conclusions on the basis of her Milwaukee show, especially to young women, who easily dominated the audience. Of course that generalization may not necessarily hold. At one quiet juncture between songs when Vega, apparently stunned by the enthralled silence of the crowd, asked if people were having a good time, a young man seated near the back yelled, "I love you, Suzanne!"

Musically, the performance was solid. Taking its cue from Vega, the band avoided flashy showmanship and concentrated on album-perfect music. Occasionally the band overpowered Vega's soft voice and guitar, and I'm sure many others in the audience were thrilled when she gave the band a break to perform the lyrical "Gypsy" alone with her guitar, just like the old days.

Vega closed the concert with two encores, "Marlene on the Wall," with her full band, and then a hypnotic rendition of "Night Vision" with Vega on guitar and Anton Sanko on synthesizers. As the house lights came up, the musical reprise from "Tom's Diner" played softly through the speakers, and the crowd wandered happily into the warm Milwaukee night.

"There's a need, I think, in America to simplify things, and to make them happy and end nicely. We all watch television as our norm, in a way, and if you start thinking that life is like *The Mary Tyler Moore Show* and it's wrapped up in half-hour segments, you lose a sense of perspective, you distort your reality. I think that's partly where mental illness comes from, because of this pressure to be happy or to tie everything up with a nice bow. Then when life isn't like that, you don't know how to deal with it. You just break. So this is my way of dealing with it . . . in my songs."

First published in *Clockwatch Review*, Volume 4 No. 2, 7-14-87/8-9-87